How to Self-Publish A Magazine
Written by Aaron Robinson and Mozella Malone

Robinson and Malone Publishing, LLC
Contact: (312) 715-7884

Published 2018 by Robinson and Malone Publishing, LLC

ISBN-13: 978-1726309387
ISBN-10: 172630938X

Copyright © 2018 by Aaron Robinson and Mozella Malone
Cover Design by Aaron Robinson
Art Direction by Aaron Robinson
Edited by Tocarra Eldridge-Robinson

The information presented in this book solely and fully represents the views of the author as of the date of publication. Any omission, or potential misrepresentation of, any peoples or companies is entirely unintentional. As a result of changing information, conditions or contexts, this author reserves the right to alter content at their sole discretion impunity.

The report is for informational purposes only and while every attempt has been made to verify the information contained herein, the author assumes no responsibility for errors, inaccuracies, and omissions. Each person has unique needs and this book cannot take these individual differences into account.

All rights reserved. It is illegal to copy, distribute, or create derivative works from this book in whole or in part. No part of this book may be reproduced or transmitted in any form whatsoever, electronic, or mechanical, including photocopying, recording, or by any informational storage or retrieval system without expressed written, dated and signed permission from the author.

TABLE OF CONTENTS

Getting Started – 8
Create Content – 13
Magazine Sections – 17
Design and Layout – 20
Editing and Proofreading – 24
Designing a Mockup or Dummy – 28
Frequency of Publication – 30
Business and Legal – 35
Production: Print Vs. Online – 41
Launch – 45
Reaching the Readers – 47

About the Authors

Aaron Robinson Biography: Editor and Publisher of Consciousness Magazine:

Aaron Robinson is the Chief Executive Officer of Robinson and Malone Publishing, LLC, which produces the national magazine titled Consciousness Magazine, as he has the creative role as Editor/Publisher for over 14 years. He is the art director of Allezom International Magazine and ultimately assists with the development process of numerous publications around the world.

Robinson attended Columbia College Chicago, holding a Bachelor's degree in Fine Arts and Science and an Associate's degree in Fine Arts. He has nearly two decades of experience as a magazine publisher and over 15 years of experience as a professional graphic designer, where he designs local and national projects.

Robinson has been a guest speaker at universities, colleges and high schools lecturing on topics concerning publishing and graphic designing. He is also the founder and Operations Manager of the youth nonprofit organization Still I Rise and holds a seat on the Developing A Neighborhood Master Plan board in his local community. As a businessman, he continues to collaborate on various business ventures, striving to be diverse as an entrepreneur, making a substantial contribution to the art and publishing world as an innovator and philanthropist.

Mozella Malone Biography: Editor and Publisher of Allezom International:

While building knowledge from professionals in the field after attending Olivet Nazarene University for Business Management, as well as continuing her education at L.A. Mission College located in Los Angeles, California, it was evident that Mozella Malone's talent would elevate her to a level of high success. Having a background in community outreach, business, publishing, education and marketing, Mrs. Malone has become known and respected for her work in the field. Over the past decade of being highly resourceful and creative, she has accumulated professional experience as a freelance event coordinator, bridal consultant and fashion designer, partaking in numerous events throughout the country. She also has worked in the Public Relations field as a devoted publicist for established businesses and individuals.

Mrs. Malone is also a Visionary. Her expertise and captured visions has allowed her to help build and brand organizations and businesses. She has also helped to establish several magazines. When it comes to social networking and developing ideas, her well-rounded knowledge of social media has given her the opportunity to correspond as a consultant for numerous companies.

Acknowledgements

I would like to thank my wife Tocarra Eldridge-Robinson, my business partner and sister Mozella Malone for being there by my side as we continue to produce the nationwide publication Consciousness Magazine. I thank Mr. and Mrs. Lee M. Harris, Michael Clark, Mitchell Logan, Hector De La Rosa, Eric Plaut, William Rasmussen, Howard Harris, Russell Norman, Howard Hogue, Dr. Shanessa Fenner and Eugene Stanley for assisting me on my journey as a magazine publisher. I sincerely thank my parents, sisters and brothers, friends, family and business associates. I give a special thanks to my fine arts and graphic design teachers, instructors and professors. I give a forever thanks to the late Sheinfield Dee for teaching me how to write and take challenges. –Aaron Robinson

Thanks are due to Aaron Robinson, Founder and Chief Editor of Consciousness Magazine for allowing me to labor beside him in birthing his publication and for writing this guide. Our journey as editors has been a long one but well worth the challenges that came our way. I cannot express enough thanks to friends and family for their continued support and encouragement. I owe thanks to my husband Daniel and to my son Aiden for their continued and unfailing love, support and patience and for putting up with my far too many side projects throughout the years. They have been my inspiration and motivation for continuing to improve my knowledge and move my career forward. -Mozella Malone

Introduction

How To Self-Publish A Magazine

How To Self-Publish A Magazine is a vital source for beginner publishers who simply have an idea, however, lack the skills, confidence, techniques, abilities and know-how regarding building an incredible magazine. This guide equips the reader with the precise knowledge, tools and resources needed to get started and to ultimately be successful by providing them with an organized easy to follow method via a preliminary step-by-step process which outlines the creative aspects such as choosing a magazine title, defining topics, creating content, developing layout and design, etc. In addition, the publication provides vivid instructions concerning how to launch, print, distribute (print or online), legalize, budget, market and sell to business customers, subscribers, and so on. Furthermore, How To Self-Publish A Magazine is helpful and useful in assisting the publisher with deciding their niche audience, as well as finding their niche in the thriving and flourishing publishing industry.

GETTING STARTED

If you haven't already done so, decide what the magazine will be about. What are the topics? What excites you? What excites your readers? While we're on that subject, decide who your readers are (also known as your target audience). Let's say your magazine is about music. Then your readers are probably music listeners!

Typically, you as the publisher also belong to your group of readers. In fact, you're the ideal and/or typical reader of that group. There are two schools of thought on that. Some people say you should write for your readers. Some people say you should write for yourself.

I'm of the latter group; I believe you should write about topics that you find interesting and exciting. The idea is that you will attract readers who have similar tastes. Don't just write basic information that your readers want to read. Write interesting and informative material that your readers should read. Be a leader.

Besides, you're the only one working on this magazine. Therefore, you might as well write about something you like. Next, decide the frequency. How often is your magazine published? Weekly? Monthly? Bi-monthly? I don't recommend yearly publishing schedules unless annual is your preference. The magazine issues will be too far apart for your readers to remain interested and gain traction.

The frequency depends largely on your motivation to be persistent and maintain a consistent schedule. Remember, you're the only one working on this. I suggest you start off with a monthly or bi-monthly publishing schedule.

Our local newspaper recently featured an area realtor on the cover of its magazine supplement. It was a large story including a photo of the female realtor on the top of the newspaper's front page - teasing the story and referring to her as a book author.

I was curious to know more about the featured realtor's book, so I checked it out. As it turned out, the realtor published the book herself, though it wasn't her original idea - however she purchased the license to the subject (how to sell your house in a tough environment) and tailored it to the area of the country she represented. But did that matter? No! The newspaper treated it as though it were any book that may have been published by a big New York City publishing house. If you asked any of her readers if they knew the difference, I'm willing to bet they wouldn't know because the information on how to sell their house was what they wanted, not who published the book!

Not long ago, self-published books were considered just a few steps above pamphlets generated on a xerox machine. How did this big change come about? Let's look at a few points:

Quality Product

The amazing changes in printing technology has made it possible for self-published books to be produced with a level of quality that can rival that of books done by traditional publishers. In the past, the look and feel of a self-published book was the telltale sign that it wasn't a "normal" book. The design (of both text and cover) was often poor and the paper sometimes badly cut. Nowadays, print-on-demand companies can offer similar, if not the same, technology used by traditional publishers and they can do so without requiring print runs of thousands of copies that often ended up unsold. Many of the designers utilized by traditional publishers also freelance their services to self-publishers. Again, the same quality and talent is available that was once only accessible to the mainstream companies.

Many self-publishing companies offer editing as a part of their packages. Present day, it's typically easy to find a professional editor for hire. This allows you to ensure that your publication reads well and is free of typos and continuity problems.

Respectability for Being Published-No Matter the Form

Many newspapers and magazines did not review self-published books, and there are some that still refuse to do so. However, currently they look at it this way - a good story is a *good* story. If your book entails a subject matter that's important to their readers or viewers (like the real estate example) or hits upon a trend currently in the news, the media would be very interested in pursuing a story on you and your publication. Again, it wouldn't matter how it was published. On television they seldom mention the publisher, and in print they note the price and publisher no matter how large or small the company.

Distribution Problems Gone

Once upon a time bookstores resisted stocking self-published books. Why? Because unsold publications are usually returned to the publisher and the store doesn't have to pay for them. Though, unsold self-published publications were unreturnable, which made them more of a risk. However, many companies have made it possible to include distribution as a part of their publishing services. That means they have worked out deals where self-published publications can be returned, making it easy for you to have your publication available in stores. Keep in mind, a store may still refuse to stock your publication, but if someone comes in and requests it, your publication can then be ordered by the store. If they receive enough of such requests, they may decide to stock it after all.

Affordability

While quality self-publishing is still an issue concerning "you get what you pay for", you don't have to spend the massive amount of money that was required in the past in order to receive a well done finished project. Many companies package their services which allow you to pick and choose what you want in the production process.

The Choice is Yours

Is self-publishing right for you? Only you can know for certain. Be sure to consider all the things you want to accomplish from being published. Is this publication just for you and your family or is it for the masses? Do you have an outlet to get the publication's message out to the public? How will you sell it? The best way for you to be satisfied with the publishing process is to be clear about what you want to accomplish and thereafter pursue the path that will get you there. Self-publishing might even be the ultimate route you're looking for.

CREATE CONTENT

Content is the key to effective marketing. This significant fact is not new, but in many cases, there is still a tendency to create content that does not necessarily attract the right customers. Content that does not coincide with your target audience is wasted content. Here are some tips to help you target and make the content you create more attractive to the people you are trying to reach.

In order to connect with the right customer you will need to first identify your customer. This may sound like an obvious statement but it is pivotal to the whole practice of content marketing. Without a clear idea of the type of people you are communicating with, where they are, and what interests them, you will struggle to create content that attracts the right people.

Once you have established who your customers are and where they are, you will know how to set the tone of your content, where to share your content and how to make your content visible to your customers. The next step is to think about what your customers are asking for and what they need.

These are very important questions that need to be answered. By answering them you will be able to very accurately target your customers. Think of it rather like a virtual target. The more specific and precise you are, the closer you will be to the bull's eye!

Take a look at your competition's content to get an idea of what they are publishing. Also, take a good look at the language they are using and start to develop your own language so that it compares favourably to those examples. Be sure to make certain you are looking at superb quality content.

Once you have answered all of these questions you will be able to develop content that will be read by the right people, every time.

Here are some examples to illustrate key points and help you develop your own content plan for targeted, customer focused marketing communications.

Organic food retailer - families, chefs, cooks, recipes, organic food blogs, recipe blogs, Facebook, YouTube cooking tutorials, food magazines, celebrity chefs, leading restaurants, and top food websites. These are simple examples regarding how you can easily build up a conceptual visual of what your customers like and where it can be found online. The beauty of this method is that it also gives you clear ideas and suggestions for the type of content to create. As you will see in the examples above, the various types of businesses have customers interested in these subject areas that are found in these respected locations. So, if they create content for these subjects and post in these locations they will be targeting the right people.

By being very specific about who you are communicating with and really learning to understand your customers, your content has a much greater chance of actually being read by them. So many companies create wonderful content that is never seen. Don't let your business content suffer the same fate.

If you effectively target all your content you will see results very quickly and the response rate in terms of visits to your website, inquiries and sales, will be significantly higher. In addition, targeting the right people will result in far more word-of-mouth and personal recommendations from customers.

The more you engage directly with your audience in this manner, the easier it will become. You will then be able to split your audience down into more specific sub-groups and make certain pieces of content even more niche.

The aforementioned technique to effectively target your content is a tried and tested method used by content professionals and it will work for you just as effectively as it does for them. Your content, to a reader, will seem as though it is talking directly to them. It will be more personal and meaningful to them.

Magazine Sections

Here are a few sections typically found in magazines. The bare minimum you should have is the cover page and the articles. There is no specific order, however be sure to use your common sense.

Cover page
This page is typically an image filling the entire page. It's the first thing a reader will see, so something interesting or eye-catching is recommended. The image could be something related to a cover story you're writing. Your magazine title is also located on this page. Choose a nice distinctive font for your magazine's title so that it will become branded in your readers' minds. Remember, your magazine title is special.

You might also want to put the magazine issue number and month on the cover page. Possibly add a couple of choice quotes from the articles within. If you're not sure what to include on your cover page, simply browse the magazine racks and look at their covers for ideas.

Contents page
A contents page shows your readers what your magazine issue has to offer at a glance. A contents page does more than tell the page number for an article, it's a quick glimpse of the entire magazine issue.

Editor's note
The note is sometimes referred to as "From the Editor", "The Editor's Desk" or "The Editor's Letter" or some variant. Basically, it's something specific that you want to say to your readers. At this point, I'm assuming you're the editor (and the photographer and designer and so on).

Maybe you want to write about the current issue's theme (if there's one). Perhaps you may desire to talk a little bit about the cover story, a significant event in your magazine's industry or maybe what you had for breakfast that day. It's totally up to you.

Readers' letters
Quite self-explanatory, publishing your readers feedback and letters (make sure you have permission) and also answering them in the magazine is another way of adding content. It shows you're listening to them, and also signals to magazine browsers that hey, there are people reading this magazine! It's okay if you don't initially receive letters from readers, simply remain focused and persistent.

Articles
This section entails normal articles, feature articles and cover stories. This is absolutely the meat of your magazine. Though, it doesn't have to consist of all words. Many magazines have a multitude of pictures.

Advertisements
This pertains to information about products and services of other individuals or companies. This may also include information about your own products and services. Don't become discouraged if you don't receive any advertisement placements initially. An advertisement is there to make something known.

Credits
If you're the only one working on the magazine, there's really no point in having a credits and contributions page. Although, if you receive input from other individuals, place their names in this section and notate what their contribution is.

Maybe you have a friend who lets you use some of her photographs or perhaps you will have several contributor writers.

DESIGN AND LAYOUT

Magazines and newspapers are essentially consumer goods, and like any consumer good, they are brands, and like any other brand they must have a logo which is known as the magazine's masthead. The masthead's role is to be recognizable. In the sea of magazines located on the newsstands, you want to assure your logo stands out. You can use basic Illustrator or Photoshop software to create the logo. When it comes to putting together the page layout, I'm sure there are numerous designing software programs out there, however, using a simple Microsoft Publisher for Windows program or InDesign software can be utilized.

As most layout editors and designers are prompt to tell you, striking an harmonious balance between text and graphics is no simple task. An ill-placed sidebar or text box can disrupt the flow of a page or even an entire article. So, where should design items appear on a page? What should designers avoid when placing text boxes, graphs, and sidebars?

Don't insert design items in places that will break the reader's concentration. Often, it is instinctive to place these items, particularly graphs, in the center of a page, surrounded by white space. A better course of action would be to keep graphics and sidebars in the margins or embedded in the text. Too much white space may distract the reader.

Design items at the end of a given article, manuscript or spread can reduce valuable sidebar and graphical content to a mere "filler" status in the reader's mind. It is important to place content within the story, preferably as close to the pertinent text as possible.

Also, add some graphical relief to your sidebars with charts, photos, etc. Sidebars that are simply large blocks of text can be visually intimidating to readers. However, be sure not to overwhelm them with oversized images either.

The most important thing to remember is that your text is the main event; all graphics should be supplementary in nature. While you want your design items to "pop", you do not want to do this at the expense of your story. Experiment with style, photos, color, etc., but do so in such a manner that will stimulate, not distract, your readers.

The logo is the most important element on the cover page. When designing a logo several things should be your concern. The logo should capture the publication's character and attitude; it should also be versatile and fit the intended readership so that it can be used effectively on various marketing materials.

When working on a logo you should try a multitude of variations. When you find several possible concepts that you like, you should work to perfect those variations. The first, and obvious thing you must do is choose the proper typography. Is your publication modern, is it more traditional, is it urban or more conservative?

Is the name of the publication long or short? If it's short, maybe you can make the logo stand in the top left corner. If it's longer and if it has two words maybe they can be positioned one on top of each other and placed in the top left corner.

If you ask yourself, why top left corner, it is because when magazines are stacked on the shelves on the newsstand, the top left position is always visible, no matter how densely stacked the magazines are. If the name of the magazine is longer you can make it a bolder type for more impact.

It is always better to use different fonts for the logo than the ones you use for the cover headlines. Although the logo is not particularly read it should be recognizable and it should be different in type from the remainder of the cover. As you can see, the options are endless.

When you finally decide on the logo versions you anticipate choosing from, try them out on the cover page to see how they interact with the images and general design. Sometimes you will find that a top left position does not work well, maybe the top centered position would be better.

Today, you can view the logotypes in almost all forms and shapes. Many indie magazines change the position of their logo from issue to issue. Most often indie magazines do not sell on the newsstands. They are distributed through other channels; therefore they have much larger freedom when designing cover pages.

Some publishers believe that "rules are meant to be broken", though the rules are there to aid you in building the identity of your magazine, which is ultimately your number one concern. However, feel free to think outside the box.

You have the option to create your logo in handwritten form, which will give your publication personality and emotion. Though, it will not give it timelessness. Therefore, you should create a more traditional logo because the modern and fashionable ones tend to last for a short timeframe.

When deciding which option to choose, always keep your magazine's content and style in mind. Use both as your guide when creating your logo. You will make your magazine recognizable and memorable if the logo compliments the style of your publication.

EDITING AND PROOFREADING

How many times have you written something, submitted or published it, then later found glaring errors in grammar and/or spelling. Maybe upon reading your "finished" product, you feel like it doesn't showcase your best talents or even worse, you realize that it doesn't even express your originally intended idea and is sorely missing any discernible closure!

It's disheartening to re-read your content and find that it resembles an unorganized jumble of unrelated sentences with no salient points to support the main idea.

What happened? You didn't mean to take the reader on a wild goose chase. When you were writing, you were excited and happy letting the words just "flow" - everything seemed so perfect before you submitted it for publishing.

1. Cool Down Period

Many novice writers attempt to write and edit at the same time. This is a mistake.

If you try to perform both activities at the same time, you will easily overlook errors. Why? Because the mindset and the skills needed for writing are not the same as those needed for editing and proofreading. One is creative, while the other is analytical.

Your state of being while writing (whether excited, sad, angry, passionate, confused, or bored) is not conducive to the cold and calculated posture you must take when editing and proofreading.

Many times, in the heat of writing there is a strong temptation to write and edit simultaneously. Fight this temptation. Tell yourself that if you try this, neither your writing nor your editing will be strong or effective.

Plan for a cool down period between writing and editing/proofreading. The quality of your writing will reflect it.

2. The Obvious

Use the spell check! It's amazing how many people overlook this initial, common sense step in editing. Due to the many factors of their computer programs, many writers simply overlook this initial no-brainer editing step.

Don't join this group of individuals as they are doomed to submitting work that is filled with misspellings, making them appear as amateurs.

With the built-in, powerful spell check function of all modern word processing programs, there's virtually no excuse for spelling errors.

It is extremely important to begin all editing activity with the spell check feature.

3. Listen to Your Draft

Spell checks cannot correct grammar, syntax, context, tone, nor the plot. The best way that I've found to check all the above is to read aloud and listen to what I've written. You can accomplish this by reading your work aloud, having someone else read it, or having your computer, via Text-To-Speech (TTS), read it.

No matter how you have your work read aloud, you can record it for later listening. This is easily done with any speaker/microphone enabled computer, modern mobile phone, or old-fashioned tape recorder.

Compared to editing by reading, listening to your work is far more effective. Errors are more easily caught when you hear what you've written as oppose to reading it.

Listening to your work will allow your editing and proofreading abilities to be taken to the next level, resulting in higher quality writing.

4. Recheck Submission Requirements

While genearl editing corrects spelling and grammar errors, professional proofreading is done to verify compliance with standards (e.g., submission requirements or author guidelines).

If you're submitting your work to several organizations (as in the case of an article being submitted to many magazines), you must ensure that your work conforms to their standards for submission.

Since each accepting organization may have their own set of standards, submission of your work can get quite tedious.

What about article submission software? I tried it once. Approximately half of the magazines that the software automatically submitted to were defunct and the rest sent me back messages stating that they don't accept articles via submission software.

In the end, I would have saved a lot of time and heartache by submitting them one by one to the different magazines.

Accept this current state of affairs. Recheck your work for conformity to each accepting organization's requirements and guidelines. If you don't, you will quickly be notified or eventually get the idea that your submission has been rejected.

DESIGNING A MOCKUP OR DUMMY

Having gathered as much information as possible in terms of design, workflow, printing, and any other consideration that should be taken into account, you're prepared to create a mockup layout.

A mockup layout is a preliminary design that accurately represents the size, arrangement, and formatting of every graphical and textual element to be included in the publication. It also clarifies the project requirements and serves as the model from which the template is constructed.

TIP

You can generate dummy text quickly by placing the cursor in a text frame and choosing Type > Fill with Placeholder Text. By default, the text is based on the Lorem Ipsum text that designers have been using for decades. If the Caps Lock key is held down, InDesign uses random words from an oration by Cicero.

To create a mockup layout, build a detailed sample document that contains the entire range of elements composing the publication's design. At this point you shouldn't be concerned with setting up the page framework, master pages, object libraries, color swatches, stylesheets, or other template elements. You'll do that in the next step. It's also not necessary to build a complete publication; however, be sure to include a sample of each page design and any possible layout variations. Do your best to make sure that all elements are included. While creating the mockup, use the project's objectives to shape its construction.

The time and energy you spend at this stage of development is an investment that will repay you many times throughout the duration of the template construction process.

FREQUENCY OF PUBLICATION

Several magazine publishers have restructured their business models through tactics such as frequency reductions to reduce costs. A frequency reduction is defined as a decrease in the number of print issues published annually, which results in an extension of current subscribers' expiration dates.

If you are considering a frequency reduction, please note the qualification and reporting impact of the subscription circulation effected.

Extension of Subscription Term

A publisher may choose to extend the expiration dates of their paid subscribers because of a frequency reduction. This is an optional strategy the publisher may wish to implement, not a requirement. The copies served as a result of the extension may be eligible for inclusion in paid circulation, provided the new expiration date is limited to fulfilling the delivery of the same number of issues originally ordered and promised to the subscriber.

For example:

• Yesterday Magazine currently publishes 12 issues per year.

• Jane Doe ordered and paid for a one-year, 12-issue subscription. She has been served five issues and has a copy liability of seven issues left on her account.

• Yesterday Magazine decides to reduce their frequency to 10 issues per year.

• The magazine may decide to extend the expiration date on Jane's account to complete service of the seven issues still due to her. The issues served to Jane as a result of the extension may qualify and be classified as paid circulation on documents.

If a publisher decides to increase the frequency of the magazine before the extended accounts reach their new expiration date, then these extended accounts must be readjusted upward so the total number of issues served reflects the increase in frequency.

If you plan to reduce your frequency and therefore extend the expiration dates of current subscribers, please notify the subscribers in advance.

Impact on Average Price

The calculation used for annualizing the average price element is up to the publisher to determine the number of issues that are going to be published in a specific one-year time frame. A frequency reduction only affects determining the annualized average price by reducing the annualizing factor used for the reporting period.

For example:
- Tomorrow Magazine planned to publish 12 issues during the 12-month sales period of July 1, 2016 to June 30, 2017.

- On January 1, 2017 they decided to reduce their frequency to 10 issues, five in the first half of 2017 and five in the second half of the year.

- For the December 2017 publisher's statement: The average price period covers July 1, 2016 to June 30, 2017.

- There were six issues published from July 1, 2016 to December 31, 2016 and five issues published from January 2017 to June 2017.

- The frequency used for the annualized average price calculation is 11 issues.

- For the June 2018 publisher's statement: The average price period covers January 1, 2017 to December 31, 2017.

- There were a total of 10 issues published in 2017.

- The frequency used for the annualized average price calculation is 10 issues.

Audit Records and Additional Cost

When subscription expiration dates are extended because of a frequency reduction, the following documents should be retained for the auditor's review:

- A mail galley for the issue published immediately before the extension expiration dates occurs. This should reflect the original expiration dates. It is preferred that this information be retained in an electronic format for auditor review.

- A mail galley for the first issue published that reflects the extended expiration dates. As an alternative to the galley, you may retain a list indicating the dates to which each subscription is extended. All typical subscription data is reviewed during the audit—original media, account history, payment, etc.

There is an additional flat fee in the audit year the extension occurs. This cost covers the effort to review the subscriber file prior to the frequency change and test the file after the change of expiration dates to ensure they were properly extended.

A Note About Double Issues

Some publishers may choose to reduce the frequency of their magazine by offering double issues.

- If the double issue will reduce the copy liability on a subscriber's account by two issues, then the frequency has not been reduced.

- If the double issue will reduce the copy liability on a subscriber's account by only one issue, then the frequency has been reduced and issues served as an extension due to this reduction may qualify and be classified as paid circulation on documents.

BUSINESS AND LEGAL

Before you start your own magazine company, online or print, you will need to brainstorm and look for ideas on the following:

1. Choose a Magazine Name

What will your magazine be called? You must choose a name that will be attractive to people and compel them to purchase your magazine.

2. Choose a Hot Magazine Topic

What will be the main subject of your magazine? Will it be a health magazine or a political magazine? Do you prefer to write about fashion or technology? Whatever topic you decide to write about, be certain to make sure it is a topic you are very passionate about and it must have a buying audience. Therefore, you will be able to create interesting and engaging write-ups that will be appealing to readers compared to writing about topics you are not familiar with.

3. Determine your Audience

You have to determine who your target audience is. What age group are you targeting? What gender do you want to write for? This is very important because it will determine the content of your magazine. The topics that may look interesting to teenagers might not be appealing to adults. Likewise, the way you would package a *men's only* magazine would be quite different from that of a female magazine.

4. Determine your Magazine Caliber

Deciding on the caliber of your magazine is an important step. Will your magazine be focused on only one area such as fashion or politics or would you prefer to create a magazine that would cover various topics? This is something you must consider before you start your magazine business.

5. Build your Content

You must take time to build your audience. Remember that you have to get people to continually buy your magazine. Unfortunately, that won't happen if your magazine is not interesting or appealing to your audience. Take time to research hot topics in the niche you have chosen. This can be done through search engines like Google and Bing.

6. Seek for Professional Help

It is important that you reach out to people who can assist you in the business. Such people may be experts in the business, content writers, publishers or influential people within your target market. This set of people would be ultimately valuable and have the ability to provide you with tips on how to run the business successfully, the challenges you may face and how to handle them as well as the ways through which you can promote your business.

7. Find the Cost Implication

Before you start your business, it is important to know how much it is going to cost you to determine if you have the required capital or would have to resort to borrowing to augment what you already have. The best way to find out if you have enough money to start your business is to have discussions with people who have experience in the business or people who work for magazine companies such as printers, writers or financial institutions.

8. Study Your Competitors

Going into a market that is overly saturated, you must make your magazine stand out from the crowd. Therefore, you have to study your competitors and see how they operate their business and what makes them successful in the business.

When you know these things, you will be able to set a higher standard for your own magazine business.

9. Write a Business Plan for Your Magazine Company

A business plan is a very important start-up tool for any serious businessman/businesswoman who desires to succeed. Your business plan contains your vision for the business and will always serve as a guide and a control mechanism for your business.

Business plans are also required by banks, financial institutions and investors when you approach them for funds to finance your business. It will help a great deal to show the financial viability of the business. However, you must make sure you consult a professional to help you write your business plan if you are unable to write it yourself.

10. Create a Great Team to Work With You in the Business

Writing a magazine is not as easy as it seems. There are a multitude of technicalities involved. You will have to produce superb articles, source for good photos and images to compliment the publication, print the magazine, sell and promote it and also manage your finances.

Putting together a magazine can be challenging. You can wear many hats; however, you cannot handle all of the roles by yourself. Therefore, it is wise for you to employ or contract other people to assist you. The assistors can be in charge of various aspects of the business. If individuals are interested in your product, they will volunteer.

A publication manager may be needed to oversee the publishing process of the magazine, a sales manager may be put in place to be in charge of sales and promotion of the magazine and a financial manager may be needed to handle all income and expenditures.

11. Source for Magazine Content

You will need writers, editors, photographers, illustrators and graphic designers to help you develop content for your magazine.

One way to reduce costs at this stage is to hire freelancers rather than full-time staff. You must make sure you select good writers who create good content for your magazine, as the success of your magazine business largely depends on your magazine's content.

12. Hire a Good Printer

When you have created and edited all the content you want to place in your magazine, it is now time to look for a good and reputable printer who will use top quality material to print your magazine and make it look colorful and attractive.

13. Plan Your Magazine Issues

When you have all the above factors figured out, you are ready to start your magazine company and release your first magazine issue.

Your first issue must be thoroughly planned out with only the best articles and photos. You should also determine the cost of your magazine and how you will be releasing it (weekly, monthly, etc.)

14. Collect Feedback

After your first issue, make sure you receive feedback and constructive criticism that will help you improve your business.

You should find out if your price is okay or if you have to reduce it to make it more affordable. What about your content? What do people think about it? You should seek out trusted people to offer you advice on how to improve what you are already doing.

15. Search for Advertisement Contracts

One major way people make money from magazines is through advertisements. After your first publication, you need to look for people to advertise in your magazine for a fee, so that you can increase your income.

The magazine publishing business is very lucrative but requires a huge capital outlay. If you do not have much money to invest, you can consider starting an online magazine which is cheaper to start and you can gradually build on that. It costs way less to set up a magazine online than offline (print). To kick start your online magazine, just follow the steps above but leave out the printing aspect of it.

Rather than print hard copies, you can set up a blog cheaply and publish your magazine content. However, I will advise you to spend some time to research and learn how online marketing works. Your online magazine blog can also serve the purpose of receiving feedback, and also a way for people who may want to advertise to contact you.

PRODUCTION PRINT VS. ONLINE

Online versus offline

I suggest the Adobe PDF file format because it works with a wide range of operating systems.

So why not an offline print magazine? It's a cheaper and faster way to distribute your magazine issues to your readers. There's no actual printing involved on your part (but your readers are welcome to print their copy of your magazine).

This saves a lot of headaches on your part because you don't have to deal with distributors, printers and other middlemen.

If at a later date, you decide you also want a printed version of your magazine, then the knowledge you receive from this guide still applies.

Web page versus file download

"Can't I just write to my blog? Why do I need to create a PDF file?"

Yes, you can write to a blog. Each article can be a single blog post. There are several blogging services which makes it easy for you to publish articles (WordPress and Google blogger). There are even free themes that you can apply to your blog so you don't have to toy around with HTML, CSS or even Javascript in order to have a beautiful website. Don't worry if you don't know what HTML, CSS or Javascript is.

A magazine should have design flexibility. A website or blog conforms to a standard template look for consistency, and requires some effort to break that consistency if you so choose.

A magazine in a (PDF) file allows an easier break. If you want an article to look different, just style it differently. You are free to let your creativity run wild concerning the design. Each and every page can be different!

"Wouldn't a URL link be easier to share than a PDF file?"

I'm assuming that in this case, you're giving your magazine away for free. Well, that depends. Facebook and Twitter makes it easy to share links. You can also send a URL link in an email, and not attach a file.

However, let's think about retention. Your reader may click on a link to your magazine article on your website or blog. They may find it interesting, and bookmark the URL. There's even a possibility that they may even share the link with their friends.

Though, a PDF file on the other hand, stays on your reader's computer. Your reader "owns" a copy of the magazine, and not just a link to somewhere in the wide world of the web. There's permanent nature to it. Once a file is downloaded to your reader's computer, it will stay at it appears. Your reader won't have to worry about the website or blog being down, or that the article was changed by the editor or writer.

"Wouldn't web pages have better SEO? A PDF file means Google can't see it."

As far as search engine optimisation goes, yes, web pages of your magazine will be easier found by search engines such as Google and Bing. From my experience, the PDF's stored on my blog get discovered by other websites looking for freely downloadable PDF's. The blog might not be listed as the source, but the search engines will eventually find them.

"What!?! I'm not even listed as the original creator of the magazine?"

As far as website and PDF piracy is concerned, assume it will be done, no matter what safeguards you put in place. The key is to make your magazine identifiable with you even when pirated or stolen.

"Can't I use one of those magazine publishing websites?"

Of course you can. You will also learn that they require you to upload a computer file, such as Microsoft Word or Adobe PDF file.

Sure, that magazine website shows your magazine in a nice user interface, complete with zooming and page flipping animations. You should also know that they basically own your magazine. Where do readers go to read your magazine? Their website. What's the link you will use to spread the word about your magazine? A URL on their website. What will your readers see while reading your magazine? Their website displaying your magazine.

There are advantages to using those websites. They usually have social interaction built in; readers can share issues, articles and talk among each other. There's also the nice user interface I mentioned earlier. The website will have a huge readership base, so your magazine can be discovered by new readers easily.

LAUNCH

Your new product has been designed, tested and packaged. Now, how do you get it into the customers' hands? With more marketing channels than ever before, it can be difficult for a small business owner to decide where to start.

Research your industry and create a marketing plan based on your insights. Winning product launches include a strong marketing campaign using a variety of marketing channels consistently and frequently.

Be sure to make a budget for launch expenditures. Set aside a portion of your resources to create professional promotional materials in multiple formats for distribution to different outlets. This may include a media kit, brochures, sell sheets/rate card, videos or press releases. Make sure you provide a consistent message in all of your materials and that your product is positioned effectively. A confused buyer will not purchase your product. It shouldn't take a lot of effort from your customers to understand what your product does and how it will benefit them.

Consider offering a special offer or bonus at launch time to get customers excited and to create an extreme amount of demand for your new product. Confirm that customers can order with ease and that the ordering system has been thoroughly tested. You should expect a heavy volume of orders at launch time and must be prepared to handle them efficiently. A customer who has a difficult experience with the first purchase may not return to make a second.

Industry research mixed with effective positioning and the right marketing channels will get your product in the hands of the customers you designed it for. Product launches are exciting for everyone involved and can really put a product on course for continued success when done correctly.

REACHING THE READERS

When magazines first became an advertising medium, and for a long time afterwards, it was assumed that each publication had a core audience consisting of subscribers or single copy buyers, which was best reflected by monitoring the size and quality of its circulation. Once magazines began to be audited by the Audit Bureau of Circulations, their claims about the number of copies could be accepted.

Reach more people with your online magazine

The most obvious channel for distributing your digital magazine is e-mail. You can send your readers an invitation to open your magazine. In this section I will give you tips for reaching a bigger audience and promoting your magazine more than once.

Successful email marketing

Various essential factors have an impact on the success of an e-mail campaign. When I say success, I mean a high delivery rate, high click-through rate and open-ratio.

Quick tips to improve your e-mail marketing:

• Write catchy email subject lines: The subject line is the first trigger for opening an e-mail. Keep it short and place the most important words in front. Make an offer. Make a promise or create expectations. The best advice, however, is to try things out for yourself. Try different subject lines and analyze the open ratio and click-through ratio.

• Make it personal: Personalize your email. You can personalize in the subject line, the content or the header image.

• Generate referrals to your magazine.

• Offer your recipients different options for opening your magazine. For example: a text link in the first line, a cover image of your magazine, a button with 'open magazine' and a list of issue highlights.

• Based on the content of your magazine, your recipient will make the decision whether to open or not to open your magazine. A single topic is unlikely to trigger people. Mention your magazine's highlights in your e-mail and refer to specific pages.

• Optimize your mailing for mobile: You can optimize your mailing for mobile in a couple of ways. Use a single-column layout and a header image.

Recycle your content

I think it's a shame to only promote your magazine once after putting so much time and effort into creating it. Plan on a second and even a third promotional push. Re-send your e-mail after a week to recipients who haven't opened it yet.

Measuring online success

If you're using e-mail software, you will more than likely be able to consult all sorts of statistics. Check the following mailing stats:

- Percent delivered
- Open rate
- Click rate
- Clicks per link
- Click through rate for magazine
- Failed

You can create UTM (Urchin Tracking Module) codes with Google Analytics to track your URLs. Insert a UTM code in every link. You can use an easy tool for setting up your UTM code. This makes it easy to track your recipients and see if they are contributing to your targets. Good luck with your e-mailings!

You want to make money from your magazine. Some of the magazine publishing websites allow you to charge readers; the feature is built in. Others allow you to put in advertisements selected by them. Pressmart does both.

You can use various host such as Godaddy or e-junkie to host your magazine file. The appropriate websites offer secure file downloading, easy management interface and integration along with payment systems to receive payments.

If you want to use a e-commerce shopping cart available with web hosting, that's fine also.

What you'll need

- web hosting and domain name
- FTP software
- word processor
- image editor
- camera or camera phone

Web hosting and domain name
You're going to need a place to store your magazine online. A website or blog of your own is ideal, since you have the most control. This allows you to market your magazine however you want. A domain name (such as thisismymagazine.com) is better for establishing a brand image.

Roughly, you can receive good hosting solutions for approximately $8 dollars per month, and the domain name is about $12 to $16 dollars per year. Web hosts typically give you an option to pay for a 1 or 2 year plan. If you choose to pay the hosting fee for the entire year, a discount is usually provided, so you will save lots of money.

If you choose the free route, I suggest WordPress.com or Google Blogger, which offers a blogging solution as well as a small web hosting solution. However, don't mix that up with wordpress.org, which offers the blogging software to install when you have your own website.

FTP software
You also need an FTP software to upload your magazine files which is really easy to use. You can use FileZilla, a free FTP software. Your web host might also have a user interface for you to upload files.

Word processor
Some publishers may use Microsoft Word together with the Save As PDF or XPS Microsoft Office add-in. You will most likely already have your own favorite word processor. Just make sure you can export or save as a PDF file.

You may be able to download a free word processor on the website. If you happen to have Adobe Acrobat, you can write directly into a PDF file.

Image editor
Although it's not strictly necessary, your magazine is going to look very bland if there is only text. Even if you're highly creative and can do all sorts of textual acrobatics with fonts, highlights, bolds, italics and text colours. Unless of course, that's the point of your magazine.

Your computer will most likely come with a basic image editor. Windows comes with the Paint program. Don't dismiss it, the Paint program that's in Windows can still create interesting graphics. The calligraphic pen tool has interesting applications. Basic Photoshop software is fine also. However, you're welcome to use state-of-the-art Photoshop software if you choose to do so.

Camera or camera phone
This is not strictly necessary, but it's an easy way to gather pictures. No worries, you do not need to be an expert photographer. Hopefully, the majority of the photos will have great quality with basic equipment.

You don't need an expensive camera. I believe that it's the person, not the tool, that determines the basic quality of the photo. If your photos don't turn out as well as it was shot feel free to use the image editor to fix minor issues.

Building a magazine may be challenging; however, with the correct resources you can turn your magazine into a reality. Remember, you can do it!

Robinson and Malone Publishing, LLC
Contact: (312) 715-7884

www.ingramcontent.com/pod-product-compliance
Lightning Source LLC
Chambersburg PA
CBHW071438220526
45469CB00004B/1579